From MILLPORT to ETERNITY

From MILLPORT to ETERNITY

Poems

IAIN FORBES

Copyright © Iain Forbes.

All rights reserved. No part of this book may be reproduced in any form or by any electronic or mechanical means, including information storage and retrieval systems, without permission in writing from the publisher, except by reviewers, who may quote brief passages in a review.

ISBN: 978-1-63684-583-8   (Paperback Edition)
ISBN: 978-1-63684-584-5   (Hardcover Edition)
ISBN: 978-1-63684-582-1   (E-book Edition)

Book Ordering Information

Phone Number: 315 288-7939 ext. 1000 or 347-901-4920
Email: info@globalsummithouse.com
Global Summit House
www.globalsummithouse.com

Printed in the United States of America

Contents

1) Houses 1
2) Our telly Life's 3
3) How long 5
4) What a laugh 7
5) Spirit 9
6) Elfin tree 11
7) Shapes 13
8) Looking glass 15
9) Set free 17
10) Trapped 19
11) Who is the thief that stole the past? 21
12) Cooki's sweet pattooty 23
13) Nice people, Bad People 25
14) Despair 27
15) Apocalyptic neurosis 29
16) Alone with the dead 31
17) The Author 33
18) The Unknown Warrior (2nd World War.) 35
19) To a Terrorist 37
20) Sermon on the Mount, or Cursed are the Peace Makers 39
21) To end all wars 41
22) Requiem 45
23) Wisdom's truth 47

1) Houses

This house is like my life,
only me in it,
I need a phone to make contact,
If only I had a number,
Or someone would call me,
Although all my old friends are still around,
They have left me,
"They attack me with their absence.".
When they were empty,
I was their piggy bank,
But now that I am empty,
They have left me smashed and broken,
But I shall put the pieces back together,
Next time I'll be more choosy,
"I won't let it happen again.".

2) Our telly Life's

Same switch another day,
The world in a box,
At the control of our fingers,
We let it into our homes.
We choose the little snippets,
Written and edited for us,
"Our choice, given by others.",
"We can only
choose what we're given.".
we all know so much now,
Since the great invention,
We don't even have to think any more,
Knowledge packaged and handed to us.
It's crazy, we don't really want the truth,
They know what we want and it's not that,
It never has been,
Every one's truth is different,
So, it's easy to give it to us in little bits.

3) How long

My dog is laying down looking at the floor,
Silently she frowns,
And the cats in his armchair world,
I change the channels but not the telly,
"What's the point?",
"All telly's show the same….".
This only goes to show,
that as things change,
It only hides, "We are all deluded.".
This constant progress,
Is just more of the same,
And most are drawn in.
Whilst I (Like the cat and dog.),
Just look on and wait,
For something real to happen.

4) What a laugh

This sadness hidden within me,
Concealed from the outside world,
by pathetic false confidence,
"What really is sad is,
I'm the only one who knows it.".
I, who show no sign of loneliness,
Strong, certain in the weak liars success,
"It's only there to protect me.",
To drop my defence,
Would let in all that I fear,
Then everyone would see my incompetence.
How am I to solve this dilemma?
"Can it be done?",
Do I accept what looks like the inevitable?
Am I strong enough to drop my defences?
Or am I too weak?

5) Spirit

Ah! Peace at last,
No more hate, or fear,
Nothing left to supress our spirit,
We can sing like the wind,
And dance wildly like the leaves,
That are set free,
From the dull life of a tree.
When a man's work is done
He becomes like a leaf,
But where is the wind he needs?
To thrash him around Wildly,
before it lays him to rest.
Why?
In his spirit, Where else?

6) *Elfin tree*

Elfin tree, the darkness has forced the last
rays of sun,
From the twilight sky,
And my spirit,
Yearns to fly freely with yours,
In the clearness of this young night,
Drawn by the timeless stars,
Down the ancient pathways,
To your world,
Your world is mine,
All spirits are one,
We spirit are prisoners,
Of a solid dream (Trapped in this World.),
Let us awake now that the sun has gone,
For it is the sun that steels our power,
We are slaves of the shining day,
The material world is dead without it,
When the sun is gone and all is darkness,
We spirit shine so strongly,
Our bodies and this world cannot hold us,

7) Shapes

Brainwashing is for our own good,
Reality can be very Painful,
It's true you have to be cruel to be kind,
For if you're weak,
Reality can be hurtful.
The mind reaches out,
To grasp the spinning shapes,
They're all there,
Right number, right shape, right place,
But something is very wrong indeed,
Is it just me?
Or does everyone think so?
We all see what is going on,
but Why do we all tell it different?
The same thing,
There is no such thing as brainwashing,
it's all lies, even the truth.

8) Looking glass

Once upon a looking glass,
I saw a sad man's face,
The people in the street below,
Were living at an increased pace,
The clock on the wall was ticking.
As time flew quickly past,
But time for him was standing still,
As he stared in the looking glass.

9) Set free

Tick tock tick tock,
Thick talk, quick talk,
There is no reason,
Or no rhyme,
For unknown words,
Set free by time.

10) Trapped

The passed is a prisoner,
The future the great emancipator,
trapped by what has happened!
The future holds no forbidden pathways.
All our freedom to choose,
But all lead to a final conclusion,
Freedom is blind hope,
Freedom is no guarantee of release,
Just more opportunities to move on,
To another finally.
Once there,
Everything is spent/ empty,
Just another cell,
The cell is inside,
We carry our own prisons around with us,
Where ever we go,
We carry our past.

11) Who is the thief that stole the past?

Who is the thief that stole the past?
And left us nothing but emptiness,
the future we have to fill,
But we only have so much future,
And in the end,
Even that is taken,
The present is the only reality,
And is truly ours,
And lives on in our memories,
In our telling's,
Is the way we pass it on,
To the unborn,
They will be "Our." future,
Denying the thief,
That past will live on,
Connecting through us,
To the future,
Which makes humans so essential,
A right to be proud,
And why we exist and know.

12) Cooki's sweet pattooty

He looks down, crouches,
Eyes are fixed, (He stares.),
Turns, ears up, and waits,
Looking down into the green,
He is surrounded by the life he will kill,
But which one?
What he does is innocent (He kills as a child.),
In his small world, these creatures are not he,
His mind is mercifully his own,
What is an insect here or there?
Compared to the synthetic wearing vegans,
The destroyers of (Entire eco systems.),
And life they support,
Do gooders my cats sweet pattooty,
He is a good killer,
For fun, he does his work,
He is not miserable,
He is not clever, or stupid enough,
To think he knows what he is doing,
He just does what he's s'posed to,
Trouble is, most of us haven't got a clue.

13) Nice people, Bad People

Nice people can afford to be!
They have plenty of money,
they don't get pushed around.

They are fit and healthy,
Have jobs, Live in nice houses,
They're nice people.
Nice people are expected to be,

Respectable, keep standards,
set examples for the bad amongst us,
they are not born weak,
Or give in to temptation,
they are gods people.

Bad people thieve and kill,
and live down in the sewage waste of
Society, the policeman protects the
nice people, punishes the bad.

Bad people are weak, temptation feeds, and
grown on the poor man's lot,
the poor are satans chattels,
it's foolish of them to pray too and worship God,
God stays with his own kind,
he would not be seen dead amongst poor
bad people,
so! He sent his rebellious son instead,
and he learned the hard way.

14) Despair

I despair of the masses,
They do nothing but follow,
"It has to be said",
They need to be led,
They're afraid of responsibility,
Of being free,
Like it was bad to feel good,
You can't blame the Thatchories,
We are bred to be (Normal?).
Nurtured,
After nature has bred us,
And learn as we grow, to be the servants,
Our parents teach us to be,
They don't have to try,
They impose their master system,
As long as they are above us, they forget,
They are servants,
Not slaves,
But rewarded for doing a job.

15) Apocalyptic neurosis

Horses hoofs drumming, drumming, drumming,
through the endless night,
Am I asleep or just lying here?
Here I go drifting, drifting, drifting,
to who Knows where?
Once again, the night riders come,
And my weak restless thoughts are no match,
For their hypnotic thundering.

16) Alone with the dead

(Walking through St Mary's graveyard Potton.)

I am a child, I am a child,
Oh! Children can cry,
Why can't I?
Nothing is right,
Everything seems wrong,
Whatever has happened,
To life's happy song?
Take a look around,
At the names of the living,
Underground,
The writing,
Like eyes upon the stone,
Are the hierarchical warning,
To the vulnerable clone.

17) The Author

God writes the scenes,
The scripts we do not see,
We blindly draw out with our emotions,
The finally only he knows,
To try ruling our destiny,
denies the prompting past,
as blind as us of the future.
Straining to glimpse the unturned pages,
We discover what will be,
Looks back on the present,
This monstrous performance,
Is directed by an ingenious devil,
Continuously at odds with the author.
He enjoys (With the audience.),
The comedy of confused players,
If we knew the script,
We could be blamed,
For destroying the masterpiece written for us.

18) The Unknown Warrior
(2nd World War.)

(Body found in German bomber,
discovered with metal detector 30 years ago.)

Forty years on and your flesh has still not decayed,
refusing to disappear as easy as did our memories,
and your horrific expression has trapped your deaths cry,
And carries it forward to those children,
Who have not yet been called to fight,
Teach them well,
For it is by no mistake that your pain lives on.

19) To a Terrorist

In this crossfire season,
Can you give a reason?
Can you tell me why,
These people must die?
Can you tell this girl's mother,
Yes, you and no other,
How you blew up,
This kid and her brother?
She'll look in your face,
And know your disgrace,
Look in your eyes,
For they tell no lies,
You act like a jury,
And cause all this fury,
You cause all this horror;
they'll have no tomorrow.
Oh, please tell me why,
These children must die?

20) Sermon on the Mount, or Cursed are the Peace Makers

When there was balance,
The Jews were happy blathering at their wall,
And the Muslims were happy worshipping
their big stone,
us, we were happy believing in something
we couldn't see,
Then along came someone,
Who only believed in himself,
And said, "There is no God."
But who filled his engineered vacuum?
"He did.",
He said, "Religion is the cause of all war.",
The final insult Everyone got angry,
"The Extremist was born.",
Vulnerable the Extremist asserted himself,
As he attacked his brothers,
The wall fell down,
The stone was exposed,
And we were left with nothing,
"Except the new Messiah.",
Who told us "There is no God"?

21) To end all wars

Spoiling for a fight,
Answering the call, who will win?
It's a secret,
Behind closed doors,
It will be decided,
By corrupt committees,
By politeness,
They'll buy the result,
And every one's a winner,
Except the losers,
And that is usually us,
But who is the enemy?
Them,
Not us,
"Oops more corruption,
We think it's real,
But what do we know?
Only "Culture, civilisation.",
What we are taught.

Happy to fail,
Through a-greed negotiation,
To benefit us all,
So, we're all happy,
"Afraid." Threats, do as you're told,
Be a good boy,
They died,
French, German, and British,
Not just flesh,
But a wondress resource,
Wasted in the mud,
What might they have become,
Scientists, Economists,

Squandered by politicians,
Alive with corruption,
Of which many brave soldiers,
Became their victims.

The prize for the lies,
That covered up the truth,
Of the social engineering,
"That continues to this day.",
But as truth dies,
and freedom cries,
Blood form the red eyes,
Of all the best that died,
Now the best,
Have been wiped out,
Leaving the corrupter's unopposed,
To lie and legislate,
And make criminals of us all,
"The heroes They'd relied on.",
"What's goin' on?
There are no enemies,
Just engineered circumstances.",
"Dam politicians.",
The new religions priest.

We are the enemy,
The unthinking heroes,
The politicians Satan,
Maggie's menials,
Upside backwards logic,
So, we must be Cleansed,
Periodically purged,
For them to make their progress,
IN OUR God given world,
Be careful you are not a threat,
Or you could lose the freedom,
"We will lose it if,
We are foolish enough,
To listen to Them,".

22) Requiem

Here today,
Gone tomorrow,
No time to dwell,
On all the sorrow,
We've had some fun,
Along the way,
To help us face,
Another day,

Another day, another dollar,
And all the shit we've had to swaller.
Why worry about tomorrow,
For it's as fleeting as yesterday,
I once heard a wise man say,
Its worries are gone with one night's sleep,
So why prepare or bother to weep,
So, live your lives as best you can,
For we're all just tiny grains of sand,
If there is a great eternal plan
When life's experience has had its span,
Perhaps on reflection the past we scan,
It's the truth we'll finally understand.

23) Wisdom's truth

(Dedicated to Mum.)

Stop being clever, it's knowledge that blinds,
Behind his red cloak EVIL stomps over innocence,
He succeeds by hiding his true purpose,
EDUCATION, the road from the truth,
There are none so stupid as the knowledge gobblers,
Weak, they believe it makes them strong,
their gadgets, we never used to need
(Are a danger to us all.),
At the magician's mercy, we've become useless,
In his red cloak, he trances us with his ILLUSIONS,
We were born with all we needed and gave it away,
Now the magician with his angels rule this world,
The great EVILUTIONIST has made fools of us all,
Wisdom comes to few,
whilst knowledge any fool can learn.

www.ingramcontent.com/pod-product-compliance
Lightning Source LLC
LaVergne TN
LVHW041550060526
838200LV00037B/1219